# *Nettle* COOKBOOK

## RECIPES FOR FORAGERS AND FOODIES

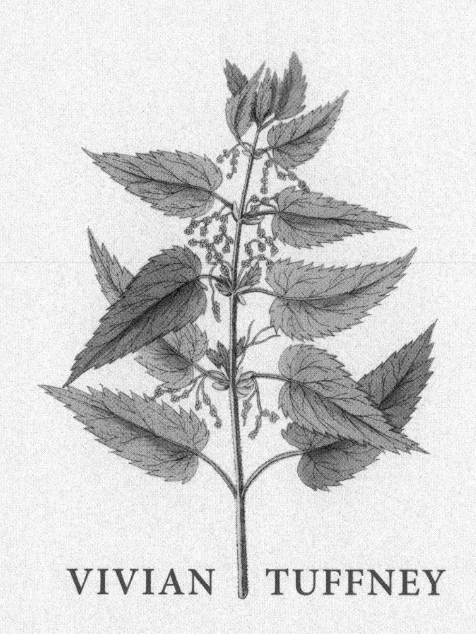

VIVIAN TUFFNEY

Published by the Natural History Museum, London

**NOTE:** If using a fan oven you will need to reduce the oven temperature by 20°C/68°F.

First published by the Natural History Museum
Cromwell Road, London SW7 5BD


ISBN 978 0 565 09355 6

10 9 8 7 6 5 4 3 2 1



A catalogue record for this book is available from the British Library.

Designed by Mercer Design, London
Reproduction by Saxon Digital Services, UK
Printed by Toppan Leefung Printing Ltd., China

# Contents

# Preface

THE NATURAL HISTORY MUSEUM held its first 'Nettle Day' in 2006. It was centred on its Wildlife Garden but extended to other parts of the Museum. Since then the Museum has celebrated this common but under-rated plant biennially with events that have included talks, displays of herbarium specimens, displays of nettle fibres and nettle dyes, and sales of plants and tempting cakes and drinks. After discussion with the Museum I started to make home-made nettle produce to sell at the events, some produce made using my own recipes and others using recipes published elsewhere, with kind permission of the copyright holder. Visitors were very intrigued to try these nettle-based foods, so much so that I was approached on many occasions for a recipe. Selling photocopies proved to be popular and inspired me to create more recipes. We came to the conclusion that a nettle-based recipe book would be a very good idea – so here it is.

VIV TUFFNEY, 2014

# Introduction

NETTLES ARE HIGHLY nutritious and grow so abundantly that ignoring them as a source of food is just wasteful. They have a high content of vitamins A, B, C and E and minerals including iron, potassium, calcium and magnesium. They also provide a surprising amount of protein. Packed with vitamins and minerals it is no wonder that nettles were widely used as a cleansing spring tonic after a bland winter diet, probably long before Nicholas Culpeper wrote that nettles 'consumeth the phlegmatic superfluities in the body of man, that the coldness and moistness of winter hath left behind'. Nettles really are a superfood – and one that is freely available. You will never have to search far to find a bed of nettles and you can enrich your diet in so many ways with their flavour!

## Biodiversity

Insects and other animals benefit from nettles too. In late summer the huge quantity of seed produced feeds many seed-eating birds. Some of our most common and brightly coloured butterflies – small tortoiseshell, *Aglais urticae*, peacock, *Inachis io*, comma, *Polygonia c-album*, and red admiral, *Vanessa atalanta* – lay their eggs on nettles. In fact over 100 species of insect, including many moths, such as the mother-of-pearl, *Pleuroptya ruralis*, beetles such as the 7-spot ladybirds, *Coccinella septempunctata*, that feed off nettle aphids, and true bugs including the common nettle capsid bug, *Liocoris tripustulatus*, are associated with nettles, and around 30 are restricted to them. So, before harvesting check the nettles for caterpillars and other insects.

Fresh young nettle growth is the best and most nutritious, so collect and cook in the spring. After this they become fibrous and inedible as a chemical change occurs in nettles around midsummer that makes them particularly bitter. However, if nettle patches are regularly mown and kept moist, they can provide fresh tender new nettles throughout the year. Cut the nettle tips (the first four leaves are best) and young nettle leaves using scissors. If you are stung, look around for large dock leaf, *Rumex obtusifolia*. You can rub this on your skin, which will ease the pain of the nettle sting. This works by releasing a moist sap that has a cooling, soothing effect on the skin. Or better still, use the juice of nettle to relieve the nettle sting!

The nettle family, Urticaceae, consists of some 2,600 species, mostly herbs or shrubs and found mainly in tropical and temperate regions. Not all species have stinging hairs, probably the minority, but all do have inconspicuous, wind-pollinated flowers. There are two species of nettle, *Urtica*, native to the UK – *U. dioica* and *U. urens*. The common nettle, *U. dioica*, is perennial and grows in a wide range of nutrient-rich habitats, including grassland, woodland clearings, fens and waste ground. It is also widespread in North America, where it is abundant in areas of high rainfall. The small nettle, *U. urens*, is an annual weed of cultivated and waste ground, which, in the UK, is found especially in the east of England. In North America, there are two annual nettles in addition to *U. dioica* and *U. urens* – *U. chamaedryoides*, the heartleaf nettle, and *U. gracilenta*, the mountain nettle. *Urtica urens* is most common in California and eastern Canada. Many people find the sting of the small nettle more painful (hence the North American name burning nettle) than that of the common nettle, *Urtica dioica*, which is used in the recipes in this book. The common nettle can be identified by its soft, dark green, serrated leaves, which sit opposite each other in pairs on the stem. It has abundant stinging hairs and when it is in flower, the greenish-white blooms are tightly clustered on elongated inflorescences towards the top of the stem. Elsewhere in the world, other members of the nettle family are eaten in various ways.

## Food

According to research at the University of Wales, Cardiff, published in 2007, 'the oldest recorded dish, more than 8,000 years ago' in the UK was nettle pudding, which consisted of nettle leaves, barley flour, salt and water blended together and added to stews as dumplings. There are even records of nettles being cultivated as an early spring vegetable. In his novel *Rob Roy*, published in 1817, Sir Walter Scott mentions an old gardener at Loch Leven in central Scotland raising early nettles under glass and preferring a variety with brown stems and dark foliage. Throughout the UK it was widely believed that three meals of nettles each spring would 'clear the blood' and ensure good health throughout the year. When we remember how, until the mid-twentieth century, there was a period early in the spring each year during which fresh cultivated vegetables were scarce, fresh nettles would have undoubtedly added nutritious variety to impoverished diets.

## Drinks

In the UK, nettle beer was a spring and summer drink, particularly popular in rural areas, and nettles remained one of beer's main ingredients right up to Victorian times. It is probable that the low alcohol content in the beer was thought sufficient to kill any harmful organisms that might have been present in polluted water. Nettles only lost their popularity as the main bittering agent in beer when new strains of hops became commercially available in the late fifteenth or early sixteenth centuries.

Large quantities of dried nettle leaves are sold for making nettle tea, but why buy the dried leaves when you can easily pick your own for free? On a dry day, after any dew has evaporated, collect young nettle leaves, dry them in the sun for 8–12 hours, turning them to ensure that they are uniformly dried, crush them and store in brown paper bags. Place a teaspoon of the dried leaves in a cup and pour on hot water. Add sugar or honey if wanted, or add a slice of lemon,which changes the colour of the tea from yellowy green to pink.

## Blanching

To retain their nutrients and flavour, nettles are best blanched. Remove the tips and young nettle leaves from their stalks using gloves, but avoid old leaves and stalks because they tend to be too fibrous. Shake off any insects. Wash the nettles several times in cold water. Bring a saucepan of salted water to the boil, drop in the nettles and boil for 20–30 seconds. Strain and squeeze off any excess water. They are then ready for most recipes.

VIV TUFFNEY AND ROY VICKERY

# Nettle Yarg on Toast

*Grill thin layers of this fresh and creamy cheese on thick white crusty toast until just melting.*

**SERVES 2**

**4 slices of bread**

**250g (9oz or 1¾ cups) nettle yarg cheese (layer the cheese as thickly as you like – you can always enjoy any leftover cheese with crackers another day!)**

1 Preheat the grill to hot.

2 Grill one side of each slice of the bread until brown.

3 Slice the cheese and layer onto the uncooked side of the bread.

4 Place under the grill for 4–5 minutes until the cheese has melted and is golden-brown.

***URTICA DIOICA*, COMMON NETTLE**

The stinging nettle is so-called because, when touched, the hairs on the leaves and stems break off and become tiny hypodermic needles that 'inject' a variety of chemicals that irritate the skin.

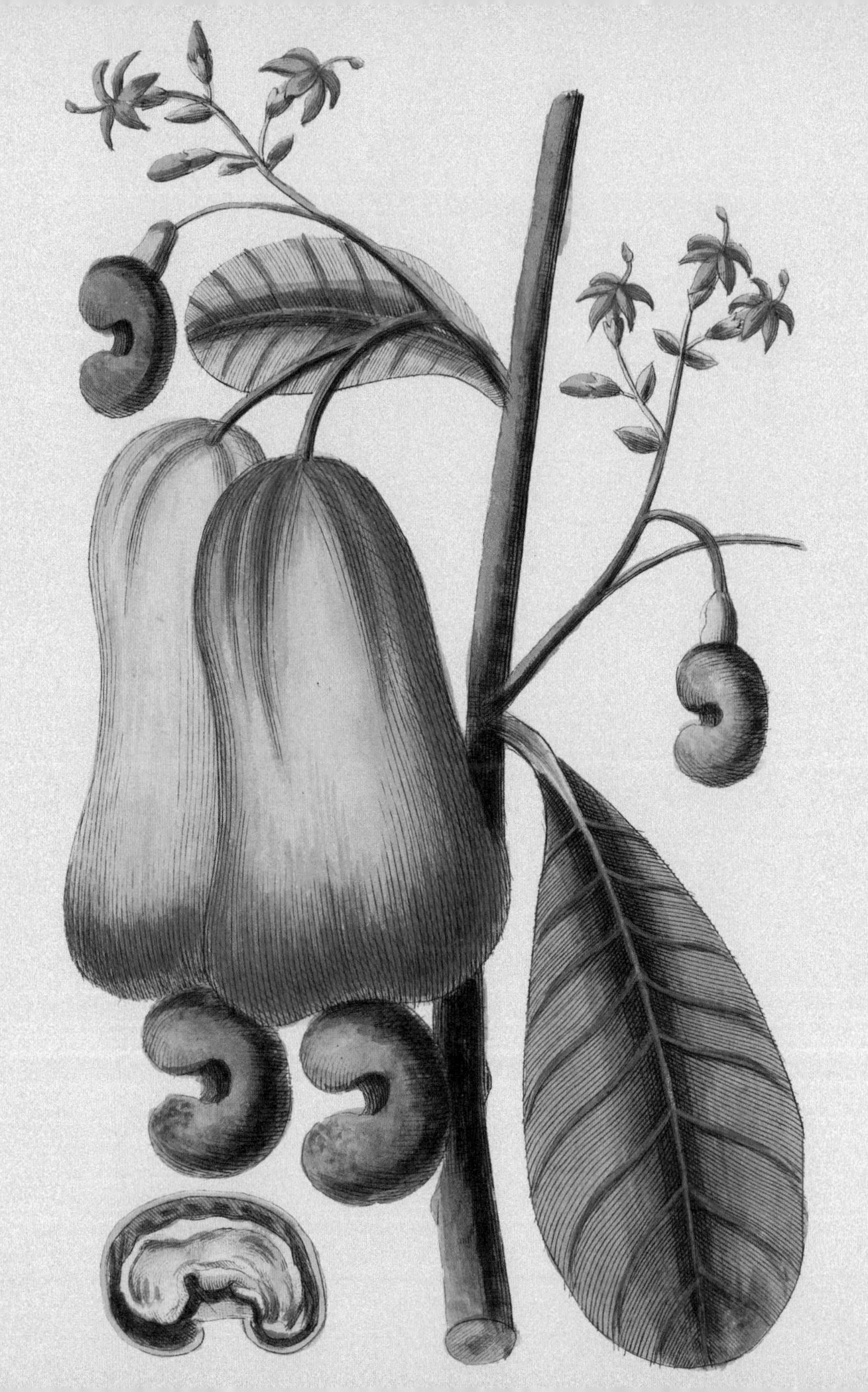

# Cashew and Nettle Stuffed Mushrooms

*Quick and simple, these delicious stuffed mushrooms are perfect served with a green salad of peppery rocket, romano lettuce and baby spinach.*

**SERVES 4**

**8 medium flat mushrooms**

**1 tbsp olive oil**

**1 medium onion, finely chopped**

**2 garlic cloves, crushed**

**50g (2oz) unsalted cashew nuts, chopped**

**110g (4oz) nettle tips or young leaves, blanched (p.7)**

**2 tsp tomato puree**

**Cheddar cheese, grated**

1. Preheat the grill to hot.
2. Remove the mushroom stalks, chop and set aside for later.
3. Heat water in a large saucepan, add the mushroom tops and cook for 30 seconds, drain and set aside.
4. Heat the olive oil in a pan, add the onion and garlic and cook for 3–5 minutes. Stir in the mushroom stalks, cashew nuts, blanched nettles and cook for another 3–5 minutes before stirring in the tomato puree.
5. Place the mushroom tops on a baking tray and divide the mixture onto the mushrooms. Sprinkle with grated cheese and grill for 5 minutes or until brown.

***ANACARDIUM OCCIDENTALE*, CASHEW**

Cashew nuts are seeds held in an outer husk of the same shape. The husk, which is never eaten, hangs at the end of an edible fruit called the cashew apple. The fruit is sweet and highly prized.

# Feta Cheese and Nettle Filo Triangles

*These soft and salty cheese-filled triangles of flaky pastry make the perfect party appetizer.*

**MAKES 8**

**1 tbsp olive oil**

**1 medium onion, finely chopped**

**50g (2oz or ⅓ cup) feta cheese, crumbled**

**110g (4oz) nettle tips or young leaves, blanched (p.7)**

**Salt and pepper to taste**

**1 packet (220g or 8oz) of filo pastry**

**Melted butter or olive oil for brushing**

1. Preheat oven to 200°C/400°F/gas 6.
2. Heat the olive oil in a pan and add the onion. Cook gently for 5 minutes or until softened.
3. Put the feta cheese, blanched nettles and cooked onion in a bowl. Mix well, season then set aside to cool.
4. Cut four sheets of filo pastry lengthways into two strips.
5. Place a spoonful of mixture onto the top edge of one strip and fold the left-hand corner over to make a triangle. Keep folding until you get to the end of the pastry sheet, and seal the edge with melted butter. You end up with a triangle-shaped parcel. Repeat for all strips.
6. Finish by brushing all the parcels with melted butter and bake for 10 minutes or until golden-brown.

**OLEA EUROPAEA, OLIVE**

Different cultivars of olives are used for oil and for eating. Green olives are unripe, those which are purple are ripening and when black the fruits are ripe.

# Cream of Nettle Soup

*Intensely green in colour, this freshly made stinging nettle soup is fantastically tasty and nutritious. It works perfectly topped with crispy pancetta or sprinkled with nutmeg.*

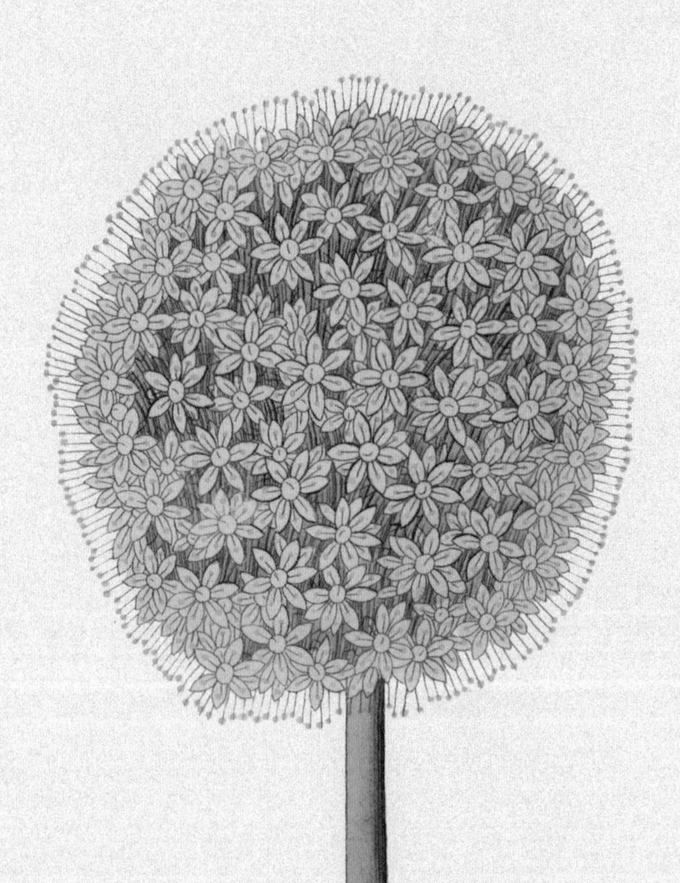

**SERVES 4**

**2 tbsp olive oil or butter**

**1 onion, minced**

**4 tsp chives, chopped**

**3 tbsp plain flour**

**560ml (1 pint or 2¼ cups) hot chicken or vegetable stock**

**500g (1lb 2oz) nettle tips or young leaves, blanched (p.7)**

**280ml (½ pint or 1⅛ cups) water**

**2 tsp salt**

**1 tsp fresh ground pepper**

**280ml (½ pint or 1⅛ cups) cream**

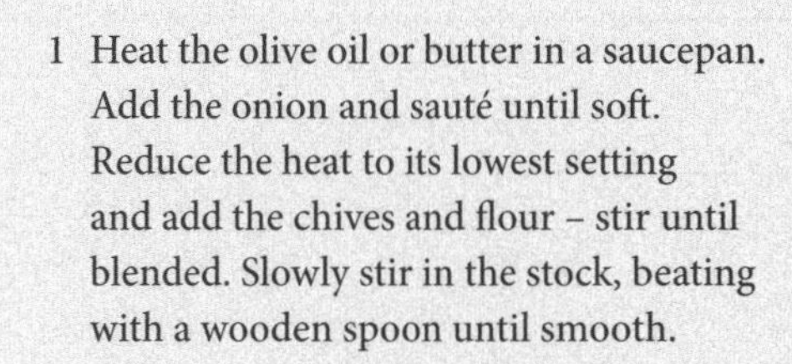

1. Heat the olive oil or butter in a saucepan. Add the onion and sauté until soft. Reduce the heat to its lowest setting and add the chives and flour – stir until blended. Slowly stir in the stock, beating with a wooden spoon until smooth.
2. Add the remaining ingredients, except the cream. Stir and heat to boiling.
3. Reduce heat and simmer for 20 minutes.
4. Add the cream, stir thoroughly and heat to just boiling. Taste and adjust seasoning if needed.
5. Pass the soup through a sieve before serving.

***ALLIUM CEPA*, ONION**

Each layer of the onion bulb is a separate swollen leaf. The bases of these overlapping leaves arise from a ring at the base of the onion.

# Asparagus and Nettle Soup

*Make the most of the short asparagus season with this delightfully smooth soup. Delicious served hot or very chilled topped with a swirl of double cream and a few drops of balsamic vinegar.*

**SERVES 4**

**1 tbsp olive oil**

**200g (7oz) asparagus tips, chopped**

**2 sticks of celery, chopped**

**50g (2oz) celeriac, peeled and diced**

**2 leeks (green part only), washed and sliced**

**3 garlic cloves, finely chopped**

**900ml (1½ pints or 3⅔ cups) vegetable stock**

**Salt and pepper to taste**

**50 (2oz) nettle tips or young leaves, blanched (p.7)**

1 Heat the olive oil in a large saucepan and slowly sweat the asparagus, celery, celeriac, leek and garlic until softened.

2 Add the vegetable stock and bring to the boil, removing any scum that forms on the top. Season with salt and pepper and simmer for 5 minutes.

3 Add the blanched nettles and simmer for a further 3 minutes. Allow to cool then liquidize in a blender and pass through a sieve.

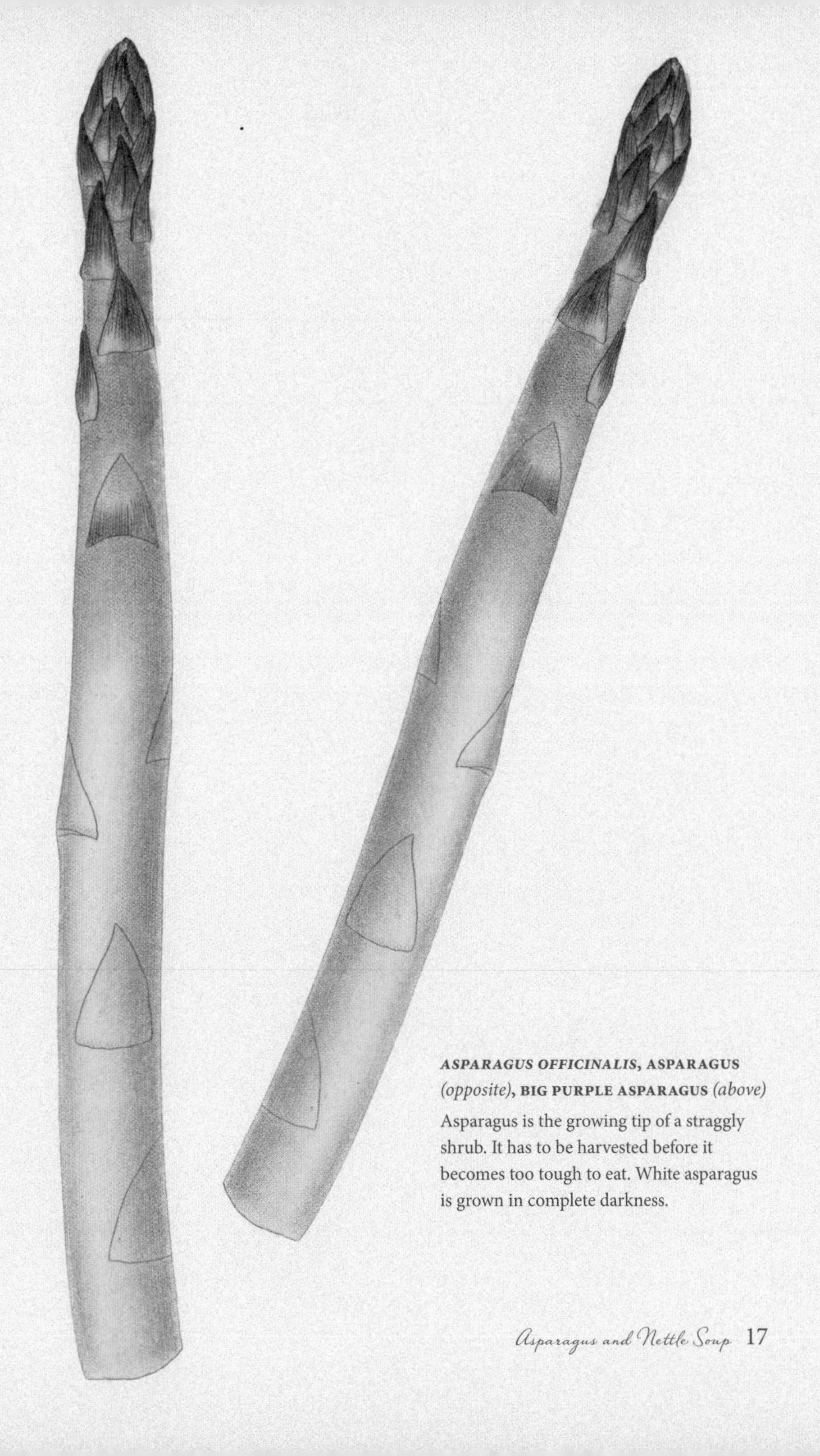

***ASPARAGUS OFFICINALIS*, ASPARAGUS** *(opposite)*, **BIG PURPLE ASPARAGUS** *(above)*

Asparagus is the growing tip of a straggly shrub. It has to be harvested before it becomes too tough to eat. White asparagus is grown in complete darkness.

# Pea and Nettle Soup

*With its show-stopping summery taste and gorgeous green colour, this healthy soup offers a refreshing light lunch or supper. Serve with a crusty slice of granary bread.*

**SERVES 6**

**4 tbsp olive oil**

**1 celery stick, chopped**

**2 garlic cloves, crushed**

**500g (1lb 2oz or 4 cups) frozen peas**

**1 leek, finely sliced**

**1.2 litres (2 pints or 4½ cups) of chicken or vegetable stock**

**150g (5oz) nettle tips or young leaves, blanched (p.7)**

**Salt and pepper to taste**

1. Put 2 tbsp of olive oil in a saucepan and heat. Add the celery, garlic, peas and leek and cook for about 5 minutes until soft.
2. Pour in the stock and bring to the boil. Once boiled, lower the heat and simmer for 20 minutes.
3. Allow to cool and transfer the mixture to a blender and blend until smooth.
4. In another saucepan add 2 tbsp of olive oil and the blanched nettles. Cook on a low heat until warmed through.
5. Add the blended mixture to the nettles and season to your liking.

***PISUM SATIVUM*, PEA 'COMMANDER'**

The pea pod is the fruit of the plant and is botanically known as a legume. Each pea we eat is a single seed from which a new plant could grow.

# Potato and Nettle Soup

*Lusciously thick and earthy, this is even tastier with a side of cheesy homemade hidgrey pidgey scones (pp.60–61).*

**SERVES 6**

**450g (1lb) floury potatoes, peeled and roughly chopped**

**1.2 litres (2 pints or 4½ cups) vegetable stock**

**450g (1lb) nettle tips or young leaves, blanched (p.7)**

**Salt and pepper to taste**

1 Put the potatoes and stock into a saucepan and gently simmer with the lid on until tender.

2 Add the blanched nettles to the potatoes, stir, remove from the heat and allow to cool. Transfer to a blender and blend until smooth.

3 Return to the saucepan and gently bring back to the boil. If it seems too thick add a little more stock. Taste and season with salt and pepper if necessary.

***SOLANUM TUBEROSUM*, A RANGE OF POTATO VARIETIES**

Spanish conquistadores first discovered potatoes in the mountains of Peru in the second half of the sixteenth century. They brought the potato to Europe, where it has since become a staple ingredient for many dishes.

# Nettle Quiche

*A crisp pastry case with a smooth cheesy filling, quiche is perfect for a relaxed picnic with friends. Serve with a French bean salad sprinkled with flaked almonds.*

**SERVES 4**

**1 pack (220g or 8oz) of shortcrust pastry**

**1 tbsp olive oil**

**1 medium onion, chopped**

**3 eggs**

**280ml (½ pint or 1⅛ cups) milk (you can add a dash of cream if you wish)**

**110g (4oz or 1 cup) Cheddar cheese**

**220g (8oz) nettle tips or young leaves, blanched (p.7)**

**Salt and pepper to taste**

1 Preheat the oven to 190°C/375°F/gas 5.

2 Line a 20cm (8in) flan case with pastry and chill for 10 minutes in the fridge.

3 Blind bake the pastry for 15 minutes or until light brown. While the pastry is cooking, heat the olive oil and fry the onion until soft.

4 Beat the eggs in a large bowl then add the milk, onion, cheese, blanched nettles and salt and pepper to taste. Pour into the precooked pastry base and then bake for 40–45 minutes.

***PIPER NIGRUM*, BLACK PEPPER**

Pepper is a vine that grows in the forests of Southeast Asia. Each peppercorn is a separate fruit that comes from a tiny flower.

# Cheese, Mushroom and Nettle Roulade

*Surprisingly simple with a wonderful aromatic flavour, this dish just melts in your mouth.*

**SERVES 4 AS A MAIN COURSE**

**50g (2oz or ⅓ cup) curd cheese**
**150ml (¼ pint or ½ cup) single cream**
**4 eggs, separated**
**200g (7oz or 2 cups) Cheddar cheese, grated**
**Salt and pepper to taste**
**25g (1oz) butter**
**500g (1lb 2oz) mushrooms, thinly sliced**
**1 garlic clove, chopped**
**250g (9oz) nettle tips or young leaves, blanched (p.7)**

**50g (2oz) butter**
**2 shallots, chopped**
**1 garlic clove, chopped**
**280ml (½ pint or 1⅛ cup) red wine**
**3 tbsp port**
**½ tsp bouillon powder**

1. Preheat the oven to 200°C/400°F/gas 6.
2. Line a Swiss roll tin with greaseproof paper.
3. Put the curd cheese into a large bowl, add the cream and mix till smooth. Beat in the egg yolks one at a time, followed by the Cheddar cheese and salt and pepper to taste.
4. In another bowl whisk the egg whites until stiff then fold slowly into the cheese mix. Pour into the Swiss roll tin and level out.
5. Bake for 12–15 minutes, remove from the oven and allow to cool slightly. Keep on the greaseproof paper and roll to form the roulade base.
6. Melt the butter in a frying pan and cook the mushrooms and garlic until all the juices have evaporated. Mix in the blanched nettles and cool completely. Unroll the roulade base and spread the mixture evenly onto it. Re-roll.
7. For the red wine sauce, melt the butter and cook the shallots and garlic until soft. Pour in the wine and port, then add the bouillon powder, salt and pepper. Reduce by half on a low heat.
8. Slice the roulade and serve with the red wine sauce.

***BOLETUS EDULIS*, PORCINO**

Porcini have tiny circular tubes from which the spores are released, rather than gills like the common mushroom.

# Nettle Haggis

*The perfect supper to warm you on a chilly night – serve with gravy, mashed sweet potato and roasted vegetables.*

**SERVES 4**

**1 tbsp olive oil**

**4 medium-sized leeks and/or 1–3 onions, chopped**

**3 garlic cloves, chopped**

**About 25–30 nettle tips or young leaves, blanched (p.7)**

**A large bowl of partially cooked oatmeal, about 120g (4½ oz or 1 cup) – this will determine the size of the haggis**

**Fresh sage, thyme, black pepper to taste**

**Fried bacon, chopped and fried or 1 medium aubergine, chopped and fried**

**Muslin bag**

1. Heat the olive oil in a large frying pan and lightly sauté the leeks or onions with the garlic. Place in a large bowl.
2. Mix all the remaining ingredients together with the leek/onion and garlic mixture.
3. Transfer the contents of the bowl into a muslin bag, create a ball and tie tightly.
4. Place in a large saucepan of boiling water.
5. Boil for about an hour, remove and allow to cool slightly before serving or leave in the fridge overnight and enjoy cold.

***SALVIA OFFICINALIS*, GARDEN SAGE**

Sage was one of the key ingredients of a potion, 'Four Thieves Vinegar', used to ward off the plague. The potion was dabbed on temples, hands and ears like a perfume.

# Spiced Nettle Meatballs

*Sprinkle with chopped parsley and enjoy with rice, a spoonful of natural yogurt and some warm pitta bread.*

**SERVES 4**

**500g (1lb 2oz) lean beef mince**

**2 medium onions, grated**

**250g (9oz) nettle tips or young leaves, blanched (p.7)**

**1 level tbsp ground cumin**

**Salt and pepper to taste**

**1 egg, beaten**

**1 large garlic clove, crushed**

**2 slices of bread made into breadcrumbs**

**Plain flour for coating meatballs**

**Vegetable oil for shallow-frying**

**2 tbsp olive oil**

**1 onion, chopped**

**2 large garlic cloves, crushed**

**560ml (1 pint or 2¼ cups) nettle stock (water from blanched nettles)**

**2 level tbsp ground cumin**

**4 tbsp tomato puree**

1 Put the beef mince, grated onion, blanched nettles, 1 tbsp of cumin, salt and pepper, egg, 1 crushed garlic clove and the breadcrumbs into a bowl, and with clean hands scrunch and mix up well.

2 Divide into meatballs, approximately 1 inch in diameter. Roll in flour and then shallow fry in vegetable oil until nicely browned.

3 Heat 2 tbsp of olive oil in a large saucepan, add the chopped onion and remaining 2 crushed garlic cloves and cook until softened. Add the nettle stock, remaining 2 tbsp of cumin, tomato puree and salt and pepper to taste. Bring to the boil, then simmer for 20 minutes or until it thickens. Taste the sauce and add more spice or tomato puree if needed.

4 Add the cooked meatballs and simmer for 30 minutes.

***ORYZA SATIVA*, RICE**

Much of the world's rice is grown as paddy rice and planted in standing water. This cultivation technique spread in prehistory from China southwards throughout the rice growing areas of Southeast Asia.

# Lemon Nettle Stuffed Pork in Cider

*Amazingly juicy and tender – best accompanied by crispy sautéed new potatoes and roasted vegetables.*

**SERVES 4**

**1 lemon, rind only**

**2 slices of bread made into breadcrumbs**

**1 small onion, finely chopped**

**25g (1oz) sultanas**

**110g (4oz) nettle tips or young leaves, blanched (p.7)**

**1 tsp oregano**

**Salt and pepper to taste**

**1 egg**

**4–6 lean pork fillets**

**Toothpicks or string**

**425ml (¾ pint or 1½ cups) sweet cider**

**4 tbsp cornflour**

1. Preheat the oven to 180°C/350°F/gas 4.
2. In a bowl add the rind of the lemon, breadcrumbs, onion, sultanas, blanched nettles, oregano and salt and pepper to taste. Mix thoroughly then add the egg and combine.
3. Make a deep cavity in the side of each pork fillet. Stuff the prepared mixture into the meat and place two toothpicks through the fillets to keep the stuffing in place, or tie tightly with a piece of string.
4. Place the fillets in a deep roasting tin and pour the cider over them. Cook in the middle of the oven for 30–40 minutes.
5. Once cooked, remove the fillets and keep warm. Add the cornflour to the cider and stir over a low heat to make a tangy thick sauce.

***CITRUS LIMON*, LEMON**

Lemons have a hybrid origin, like many citrus fruits, and are the result of a cross between the sour orange and the citron.

# Nettle Kail

*A beautifully simple chicken dish that's wonderfully moist and packed full of flavour.*

**SERVES 4**

**50g (2oz) fat (suet, dripping or butter)**

**1 medium onion, finely chopped**

**175g (6oz) medium oatmeal**

**1 tbsp spearmint, mint or wild garlic, chopped**

**1¼–1½ kg (2½–3lb) chicken**

**2¼ litres (4 pints or 8 cups) water**

**Salt and pepper to taste**

**25g (1oz) barleymeal or fine oatmeal**

**500g (1lb 2oz) nettle tips or young leaves, blanched (p.7)**

1. To make the stuffing, melt the fat in a saucepan and fry the onion till cooked but not brown. Add the medium oatmeal and cook for a few minutes. Season and then add spearmint, mint or wild garlic.
2. Stuff the body cavity of the chicken, then skewer or tie up the opening. Put the chicken into a large pot and add water, salt and pepper. Bring to the boil and simmer for 1–1½ hours.
3. When the chicken is almost cooked, add the barley flour or fine oatmeal and blanched nettles to the saucepan. Simmer for about 10 minutes.
4. When the chicken is cooked, remove from the pan allowing all the water to drain.
5. The boiled nettles can be eaten as an accompanying side dish. Remove them with a slotted spoon and place in another dish, add a knob of butter and a little of the cooking liquor.

***MENTHA SPICATA*, SPEARMINT**

Spearmint's name comes from the pointed leaf tips that are like tiny spears. It is one of the parents of the hybrid species peppermint.

# Nettle Frittata

*Great for summer picnics – prepare the night before and leave to cool, then dish up a thick slice with a chunky tomato and cucumber salad.*

**SERVES 3**

**olive oil**

**1 medium onion, thinly sliced**

**3 garlic cloves, crushed**

**Salt and pepper to taste**

**500g (1lb 2oz) nettle tips or young leaves, blanched (p.7)**

**50g (2oz or ⅓ cup) Parmensan, grated**

**50g (2oz or ⅓ cup) young pecorino or sardo, grated**

**6 eggs, lightly beaten**

1. Heat a splash of olive oil in a large frying pan over a medium heat. Add the onion and sauté until softened. Add a splash more olive oil to the frying pan and add the garlic, season with salt and cook for another minute.
2. Add the blanched nettles and turn the heat to high. Cook until most of the water released has evaporated.
3. Place the nettle mixture in a colander to drain away any excess water. When cool, chop coarsely and place into a bowl. Mix in the cheese and enough olive oil to coat. Beat in the eggs and season well.
4. Warm 1 tbsp olive oil in a large non-stick skillet or frying pan and pour in the egg and nettle mixture. Cook over a medium–low heat until just set and starting to brown.
5. Slide the frittata onto a plate and then invert back into the frying pan. Cook for roughly 10–15 minutes or until done.

***URTICA DIOICA*, COMMON NETTLE**

The leaves of nettles are high in vitamins and minerals, but are best eaten early in the season. Soaking them in water removes the stinging chemicals.

# Nettle Mash with Roast Broccoli and Sesame Seeds

*This inspired side dish combines Asian flavours with classic British foods.*

***SESAMUM INDICUM*, SESAME SEEDS**

Wild relatives of sesame occur in dry areas of sub-Saharan Africa and the crop itself is highly drought resistant. Sesame has the highest oil content of any seed.

**SERVES 4**

**900g (2lb) floury potatoes, peeled and chopped**

**½ tsp salt**

**Large handful of nettle tips or young leaves, blanched (p.7)**

**½ to 1 tbsp nettle stock (water from blanched nettles)**

**6 tbsp olive oil**

**3 heads of broccoli, cut into florets**

**3 garlic cloves, finely diced**

**2 tbsp tamari or soy sauce**

**Pepper to taste**

**1 tbsp lightly toasted sesame seeds, to garnish**

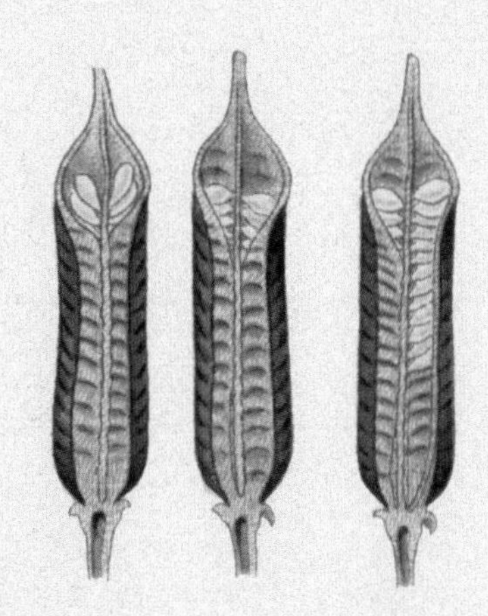

1. Preheat the oven to 190°C/375°F/gas 5.
2. Boil the potatoes in salted water for 15 minutes or until tender.
3. While the potatoes are cooking, tip the blanched nettles, a little nettle stock and 4 tbsp of oil into a blender. Blend until smooth.
4. Toss the broccoli and garlic in the tamari or soy sauce and remaining oil. Place in a roasting tin and roast for 5 minutes.
5. While the broccoli is in the oven, drain the potatoes and return to the saucepan. Put back on the hob and stir until any leftover liquid has evaporated.
6. Remove from the heat and mash with the nettle mixture. Add pepper as desired and then heat through and keep warm.
7. Serve the roast broccoli on top of the mash and scatter with sesame seeds.

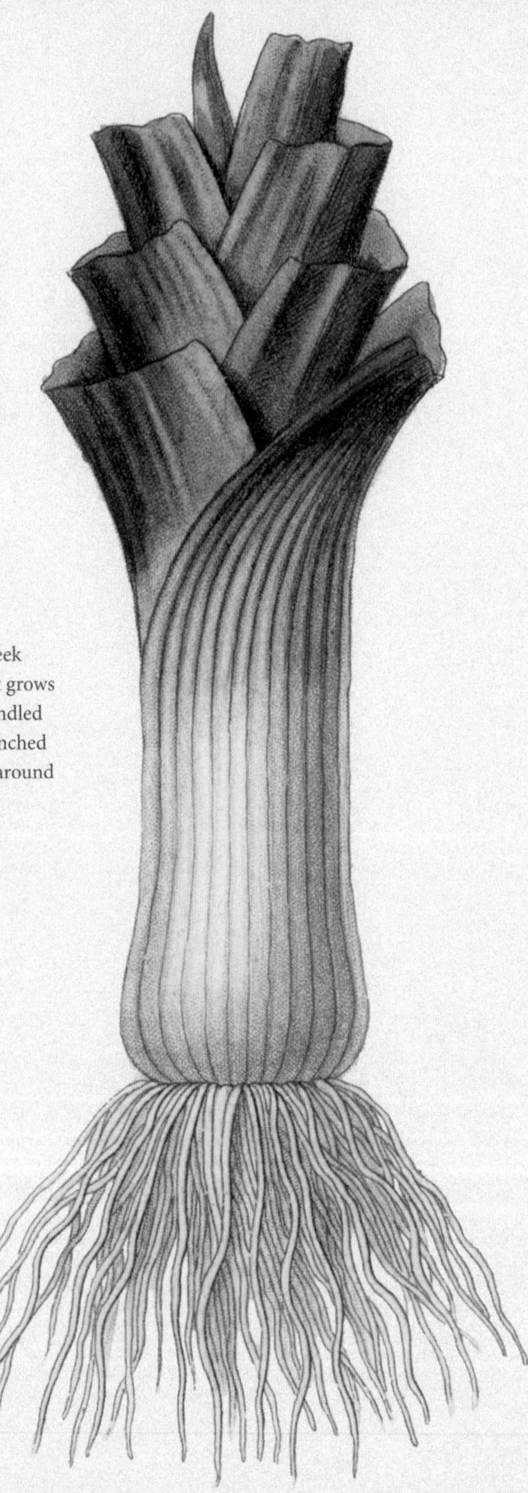

***ALLIUM AMPELOPRASUM***

**CULTIVAR, LEEK**

Unlike its relative the onion, the leek does not form a tight bulb when it grows – it produces long cylinders of bundled leaf sheaths. The leaf bases are blanched (turned white) by mounding soil around the base of the plant as it grows.

# Nettle Pasta

*After rolling, cutting and dusting lightly with flour, portion out the pasta and freeze for use later.*

**SERVES 6**

**1 tbsp butter**

**2 garlic cloves, chopped**

**1 whole large leek, chopped**

**175g (6oz) nettle tips or young leaves, blanched (p.7)**

**Salt and pepper to taste**

**2 eggs**

**3 egg yolks**

**450g (16oz or 3 cups) un-sifted plain flour**

**½ tsp salt**

1 Heat the butter in a large saucepan. Add the garlic and leek, and sauté in the hot butter for 3 to 4 minutes. Add the blanched nettles and some seasoning.

2 Cover the pot for 5 minutes to draw the water out of the vegetables. Remove the lid and continue to cook until all the water has evaporated, stirring occasionally. Leave to cool completely, then blend until smooth.

3 Beat together the eggs and egg yolks then stir through the cooked greens.

4 In a separate bowl, add the flour and make a well in the centre. Carefully pour in the egg and greens mixture and the salt. Draw the flour into the egg mixture.

5 Flour your hands lightly and knead the contents of the bowl to a smooth elastic consistency for about 10 minutes. Then, wrap in clingfilm and leave to rest in the fridge for 30 minutes.

6 Cut the dough into about six pieces and run through a pasta-rolling machine until smooth and dry, or continue to knead for a few more minutes by hand to get the same effect.

7 From here, you can follow your preferred method for turning the dough into long thin strips of pasta, either stretching it by hand or using a machine.

8 Serve with nettle pesto (p.50).

# Nettle Ravioli

*A dish for early springtime – share a large bowl of this simple, satisfying, wild ravioli with friends.*

**SERVES 6**

**50g (2oz) pine nuts**

**350g (12oz) nettle tips or young leaves, blanched (p.7)**

**50g (2oz or ⅓ cup) Parmesan, grated (save a little for tossing)**

**25g (1oz) basil, chopped**

**1 quantity of pasta dough (p.39)**

**Semolina or plain flour for sprinkling**

**Olive oil**

***OCIMUM BASILICUM*, SWEET BASIL**

Members of the Lamiaceae, or mint family to which basil belongs, have high concentrations of many types of essential oils, usually held in special cells in the leaves.

1 Put the pine nuts in a blender and blend for 30 seconds. Add the blanched nettles, Parmesan cheese and basil and process for a further 30 seconds.

2 Divide the pasta dough into four. Keep any dough you are not working with covered. Roll out the dough into a long strip 3in (7.5cm) wide and ½in (2mm) deep.

3 Arrange teaspoons of the filling 1½in apart in parallel rows on the pasta.

4 Roll out a second piece of dough slightly larger and place over the first piece. Press with your fingers around each filling to form small cushions. Cut the individual cushions out with a knife or a fluted pastry wheel. Repeat the whole process with the other two pieces of pasta dough.

5 Sprinkle semolina or flour over a clean tea towel and arrange the finished ravioli on top.

6 Bring a large saucepan of salted water to the boil and cook the ravioli for about 5 minutes or until they rise to the top of the saucepan. Remove and toss in a little olive oil and Parmesan.

# Egg and Nettle Florentine

*The perfect combination of ingredients for an indulgent weekend brunch – go on, wake up late!*

**SERVES 1**

**Large knob of butter**

**1 small onion, sliced finely**

**110g (4oz) mushrooms, sliced**

**110g (4oz) nettle tips or young leaves, blanched (p.7)**

**1 flat bread**

**Homemade tomato and nettle sauce (pp.52–53)**

**1 ball of mozzarella cheese**

**1 egg**

1. Preheat the oven to 180°C/350°F/gas 4.
2. Melt the butter in a frying pan and fry the onion for 2 minutes. Add the mushrooms and blanched nettles and cook for a further 3 minutes.
3. Place the flat bread on a baking tray and spread with tomato and nettle sauce. Top with the onion, mushroom and nettle mixture, leaving a small space in the middle for the egg. Layer some mozzarella cheese on top, then crack an egg in the middle of the pizza. Place on the top shelf of the oven and cook for 8–10 minutes.

***URTICA DIOICA*, COMMON NETTLE**

The expression 'grasp the nettle' comes from the fact that grabbing a nettle stem firmly, rather than brushing against it, flattens the stinging hairs so they cannot inject their chemicals.

***CAPSICUM ANNUUM*, CAYENNE PEPPER**

All capsicum species are native to the New World and were brought to Asia by European explorers, where they quickly became important in many sorts of cuisines. The spicy hotness of peppers is caused by a chemical called capsaicin, which activates the same receptors in the brain that respond to heat.

# Beef and Nettle Goulash

*A hearty goulash is the perfect comfort food to end a long cold day. Dish up with rice, dumplings or potatoes with a dollop of soured cream and chives.*

SERVES 4–6

**3 tbsp olive oil**

**500g (1lb 2oz) stewing steak, cut into bite-sized chunks**

**1 large onion, sliced**

**1 large red pepper, sliced**

**2 large carrots, sliced**

**5 level tbsp paprika**

**560ml (1 pint or 2¼ cups) beef stock**

**1 can of chopped tomatoes**

**Salt and pepper to taste**

**2 tbsp tomato puree**

**220g (8oz) mushrooms**

**220g (8oz) nettle tips or young leaves, blanched (p.7)**

1. Heat the olive oil in a large saucepan and fry the beef until brown. Remove from the heat and set aside.
2. Place the onion, pepper and carrots into the same saucepan and fry for about 5 minutes. Stir in the paprika.
3. Add the beef stock, chopped tomatoes and beef chunks to the vegetables and stir. Season with salt and pepper and simmer on a very low heat for about 40 minutes. If the sauce needs to be thickened, add some tomato puree.
4. Add the mushrooms and blanched nettles and cook for a further 15 minutes.

# Sausage and Nettle Calzones

*Meaty, cheesy and full of flavour, drizzle chilli oil over these tasty calzones and serve with a crunchy salad.*

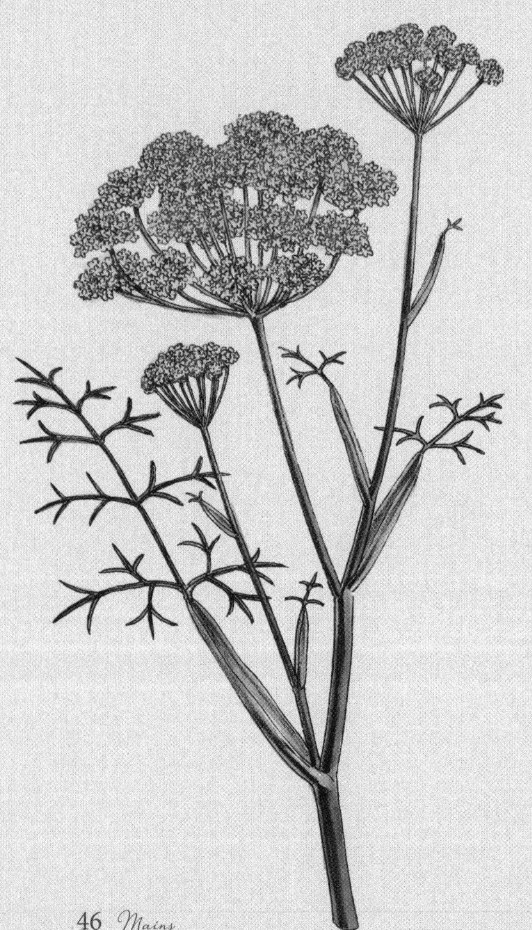

**SERVES 6**

**25 g (1oz) dried tomatoes**

**120ml (¼ pint or ½ cup) hot water**

**1 tbsp olive oil**

**6 pork sausages, chopped**

**50g (2oz) onion, chopped**

**½ tbsp garlic cloves, minced**

**½ tsp fennel seeds**

**110g (4oz) nettle tips or young leaves, blanched (p.7)**

**110g (4oz or 1 cup) provolone cheese, finely diced**

**75g (3oz or ⅔ cup) whole milk ricotta cheese**

**Pepper to taste**

**Pizza dough (p.78)**

**Plain flour for rolling**

**2 tsp dried oregano**

**1 large egg mixed with 1 tbsp water**

1 Preheat the oven to 450°F/230°C/gas 8.

2 To make the filling, place the dried tomatoes in a heatproof bowl and cover with hot water. Press the tomatoes into the liquid and leave to stand until softened for 10–20 minutes.

3 Remove the tomatoes, squeezing out any excess liquid, save the liquid for later, and chop.

4 Heat the olive oil in a large saucepan over a medium to high heat. Add the sausages and brown.

5 Reduce the heat and add the onion, garlic and fennel seeds. Cook for 10 minutes, stirring often.

6 Add the reserved tomato water and increase the heat, and cook until the liquid has almost gone.

7 Stir in the blanched nettles and cook for 2–4 minutes. Stir in the tomatoes, remove from the heat and cool to room temperature, then stir in both kinds of cheese and season with pepper to taste.

8 Make a simple pizza dough (p.78).

9 Cover a baking tray with greaseproof paper then turn the dough onto a floured surface, roll it lightly in the flour and knead briefly. Divide into six portions and roll each one into a ball. Holding one ball in your hands at a time, gently stretch each one into a 6in circle.

10 Smear the topping onto one side of the rounds, sprinkle with oregano, and brush egg mixture around the pizza edges. Carefully fold the dough over the filling and roll up the edges to form a seal. Brush tops with egg mixture.

11 Place the calzones on the prepared baking tray. Bake until golden brown, approximately 25–30 minutes.

***Foeniculum vulgare*, fennel**

The bulbs of fennel are expanded leaf bases, the leaves themselves are feathery like those of dill, but have a completely different flavour, almost like liquorice.

# *Gnocchi with Nettles*

*Especially tasty doused with plenty of butter and topped with toasted pine nuts and grated Parmesan.*

**SERVES 2**

**750g (1½ lb) potatoes**

**170g (6oz) nettle tips or young leaves, blanched (p.7)**

**2 egg yolks**

**150g (5oz or 1 cup) plain flour**

**Nettle pesto (p.50) or tomato and nettle sauce (p.53)**

1. Boil the potatoes in a large saucepan of salted water until soft. Drain, then return to the saucepan and mash together with the blanched nettles.
2. Add the egg and flour to the potato mixture and bring the mixture together to form a dough.
3. Divide the dough into several pieces and roll out gently with your hands until you have rolls about ¾in in diameter.
4. Cut the rolls of dough into pieces about 1in long. Using your fingertip, press against a piece of the dough and roll it slightly to form an indentation. As the gnocchi are made, place them on a baking tray and lightly dust with flour.
5. Boil a saucepan of salted water and gently drop the gnocchi, a few at a time, into the water. As soon as they rise to the surface remove them with a slotted spoon and drain well.
6. Arrange on a warm serving dish and serve with nettle pesto or tomato and nettle sauce.

***URTICA DIOICA*, COMMON NETTLE**

The common stinging nettle has unisexual flowers on separate plants – one plant has pollen-bearing flowers and is male, the other has flowers with ovaries and is female.

# Nettle Pesto

*A fabulously earthy pesto, perfect tossed through pasta with a spoonful of crème fraiche, or spread on toasted ciabatta and topped with feta cheese, chopped tomatoes and onion.*

**SERVES 6**

**110g (4oz) nettle tips or young leaves, blanched (p.7)**

**3 garlic cloves, finely chopped**

**50g (2oz) pine nuts**

**50g (2oz or ½ cup) Parmesan, grated**

**Salt and pepper to taste**

**6 tbsp extra virgin olive oil**

1. Whiz the blanched nettles, garlic, pine nuts, Parmesan and a little salt and pepper in a blender. Blend until the mixture is smooth, scraping down the side occasionally. While the motor is running gradually pour in the olive oil until well distributed.
2. Put the pesto in a sterilized jar and pour a little extra olive oil over the top. Seal well with a lid and refrigerate until ready to use.
3. The pesto will keep for up to a month if refrigerated in a well-sealed jar.

***ALLIUM SATIVUM*, GARLIC**

The pungent odour of garlic comes from sulphur-containing chemicals that are most concentrated in the green centres of the cloves. These compounds are also antibiotic and were used to preserve food in the days before refrigeration.

# Tomato and Nettle Sauce

*This sweet and spicy tomato sauce is great for chicken, on pizza or stirred through pasta.*

**SERVES 4**

**1 medium onion, chopped**

**1 tsp olive oil**

**2–3 garlic cloves, chopped**

**2 tsp dried mixed herbs**

**150g (5oz) nettle tips or young leaves, blanched (p.7)**

**Small tin (220g or 8oz) of chopped tomatoes**

**1 tbsp tomato puree**

**1 tsp paprika**

**150ml (¼ pint or ¾ cup) water or wine**

**A pinch of crushed chillies, optional**

**Salt and pepper to taste**

1. Heat the olive oil in a saucepan. Add the onion and garlic and fry till soft and light brown.
2. Add the rest of the ingredients, stir thoroughly and bring to the boil. Season with salt and pepper.
3. Reduce the heat and cook for 20 minutes or until thickened.
4. Keep overnight in the fridge or freeze to make weekday meals easy.

***SOLANUM LYCOPERSICUM*, TOMATO**

Pomi di oro was an early name for tomatoes. Translation to pomme d'amour and then to love apples gave the fruits a reputation as aphrodisiacs when they were first grown in Europe.

# Nettle Shortbread

*These light buttery biscuits are so easy and delicious, they will be impossible to resist.*

**MAKES 20**

**220g (8oz) butter**

**110g (4oz or ½ cup) caster sugar**

**220g (8oz or 1 cup) plain flour**

**110g (4oz or ½ cup) cornflour**

**Pinch of salt**

**3 nettle teabags, remove tea from the bags**

1 Preheat the oven to 160°C/325°F/gas 3.

2 Cream the butter and sugar together in a bowl until pale and creamy. Sift in the flour and the cornflour, add the salt and nettle tea and gently mix together. Using your hands, squeeze the mixture together into a ball of soft dough.

3 Tip onto a lightly floured work surface and roll into a sausage shape about 7½cm (3in) in diameter. Refrigerate for 10 minutes.

4 Cut into slices about 1½cm (½in) thick and place on a baking tray lined with greaseproof paper. Prick the tops of the shortbread with a fork and bake for 15–20 minutes or until lightly browned. Cool on a wire tray.

***ZEA MAYS*, MAIZE**

The ears of maize are made up of the female flowers and each kernel is a seed from one flower. The male flowers are held in tassels at the top of the plant and look very different.

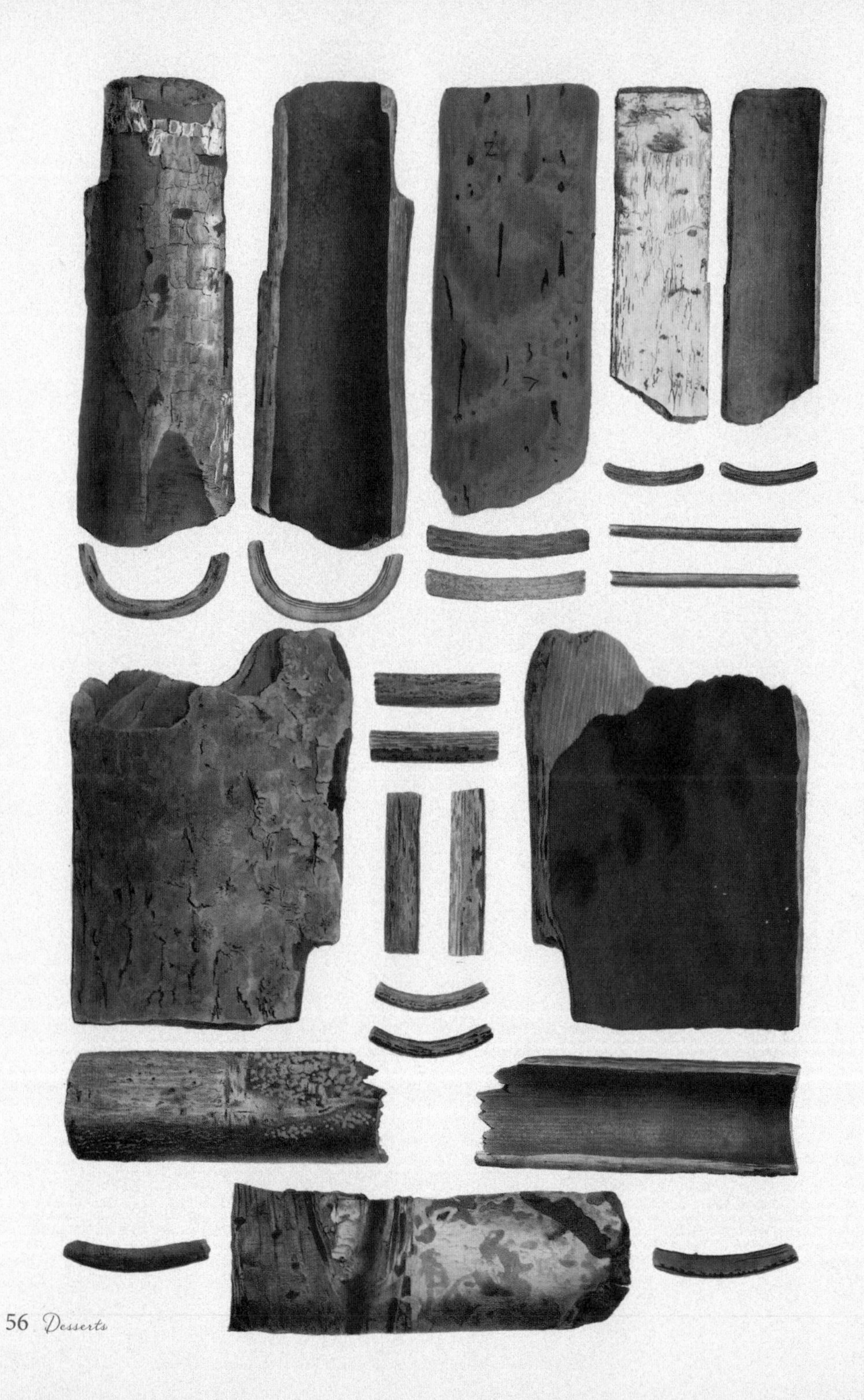

# Ginger and Nettle Biscuits

*Deliciously moreish and slightly chewy, these biscuits are great fun to make. Try adding chopped crystallized ginger to make them even better.*

**MAKES 15**

**50g (2oz) butter**
**110g (4oz or ½ cup) soft brown sugar**
**220g (8oz or 2 cups) plain flour**
**½ tsp bicarbonate of soda**
**2 tsp ground ginger**
**½ tsp ground cinnamon**
**2 nettle teabags; remove tea from the bags**
**1 egg**
**1 tbsp golden syrup**

1 Preheat the oven to 160°C/325°F/gas 3.

2 Place the butter in a saucepan and gently heat until melted.

3 Mix together all the other ingredients in a large bowl. Add the melted butter and combine.

4 Press into a ball and refrigerate for about 10 minutes. Remove and gently roll the dough out to about 1½cm (½in) thick. Cut into shapes using a biscuit cutter.

5 Transfer the biscuits to a baking tray lined with greaseproof paper and bake for 15–20 minutes. Allow to cool on a wire tray.

***CINNAMOMUM CASSIA*** *(top)*, ***CINNAMOMUM XANTHONEURUM*** *(bottom)*, **CINNAMON**

Cinnamon comes from the inner bark of several species of tropical trees in the laurel family – the trees are coppiced to harvest the bark, then they grow back from the cut stump.

# Viv's Nettle Scones

*A versatile scone – try warm with butter, or cold with clotted cream and apple and nettle jelly (p.66).*

MAKES 8

**220g (8oz or 1 cups) self-raising flour**
**2 tsp baking powder**
**Pinch of salt**
**50g (2oz) unsalted butter**
**25g (1oz or ⅛ cup) caster sugar**
**3 nettle teabags; remove tea from the bags**
**150ml (¼ pint or ¾ cup) milk**

1 Preheat the oven to 220°C/425°F/gas 7.

2 Sift the flour and baking powder into a large bowl, and add the salt and butter. Rub the mixture between your fingertips until it resembles breadcrumbs.

3 Add the sugar and the nettle tea to the mixture. Slowly add the milk and mix together with a fork. Once fully combined knead the mixture and tip onto a lightly floured surface. Roll to roughly 1cm (½in) thick.

4 Using a cutter, cut 8 scones. Place them in the fridge for 10 minutes to rest the dough – this will help the scones keep their shape while baking. Place on a baking sheet and brush with milk and bake in the middle of a preheated oven for 12–15 minutes until brown. (Don't open the oven before 10 minutes.)

***SACCHARUM OFFICINARUM*, SUGAR CANE**

Sugar cane is a grass that can grow up to 3m (10ft) tall. The sugar syrup is squeezed from the thick stems, which in Guyana are called 'bagasse' and are used to power the furnaces that boil down the syrup to form sugar crystals.

# Hidgrey Pidgey Scones

*A mouth-watering savoury scone – best eaten warm spread liberally with butter.*

MAKES 8

**220g (8oz or 1 cup) wholemeal plain flour**

**¼ tsp salt**

**1 nettle teabag; remove tea from the bag**

**110g (4oz) unsalted butter**

**110g (4oz or ½ cup) Lancashire cheese or hard crumbly cheese**

**1 egg**

**150ml (¼ pint or ¾ cup) milk**

1. Preheat the oven to 200°C/400°F/gas 6.
2. Sift the flour into a large bowl and add the salt and the nettle tea. Mix well.
3. Rub in the butter using your fingertips until the mixture resembles breadcrumbs.
4. Crumble in the cheese, followed by the egg and then the milk. Mix with a wooden spoon to form a firm dough.
5. Shape into 8 round scones.
6. Place on a baking tray lined with greaseproof paper and bake for 25 minutes until brown.

***URTICA DIOICA*, COMMON NETTLE**

The common nettle can be difficult to remove from gardens as its underground stems (or roots) can spread to several feet.

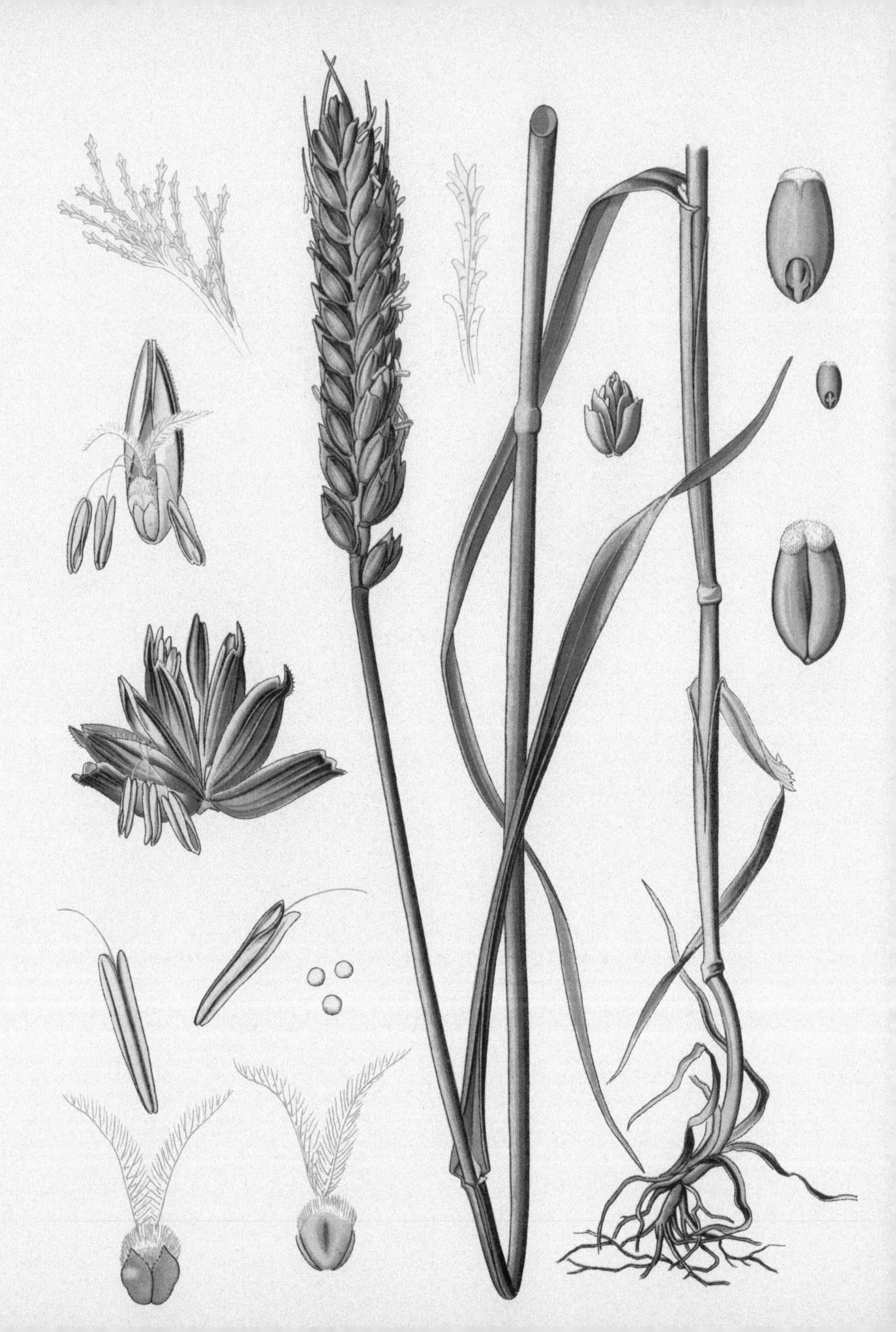

# Victoria Nettle Sponge

*A classic Victoria sponge with an artisan twist.*

**SERVES 8**

**220g (8oz) butter**

**220g (8oz or 1 cup) caster sugar**

**2 eggs, beaten**

**220g (8oz or 1 cup) self-raising flour**

**2 tsp baking powder**

**3 nettle teabags; remove tea from the bags**

**4 tbsp apple and nettle jelly (pp.66–67)**

**150 ml (¼ pint or ¾ cup) whipped fresh cream**

***TRITICUM AESTIVUM*, COMMON WHEAT**

Wheat was domesticated from a hybrid wild grass whose ears became non-shattering. This meant that the seeds (grains) stayed on the plant, allowing people to harvest them more easily.

1. Preheat the oven to 180°C/350°F/gas 4.
2. Line two 18 or 20cm (7 or 8in) sandwich tins with greaseproof paper.
3. Cream the butter and sugar together in a large bowl until light and fluffy.
4. Slowly stir in the beaten eggs and then fold in the flour, baking powder and nettle tea.
5. Divide the cake mixture evenly into both tins and place in the middle of the oven for approximately 25 minutes or until golden and the cake springs back when pressed. (Try not to open the oven door during the baking or the cake will sink in the middle.)
6. Leave to cool for 5 minutes then tip out onto a wire tray to cool. When completely cool sandwich the two cakes together with the apple and nettle jelly and cream.

# Nettle Ice-cream

*A delightful light green, dreamy, creamy treat.*

**SERVES 4–6**

**110g (4oz or ½ cup) golden caster sugar**

**4 egg yolks**

**1 tsp cornflour**

**280ml (½ pint or 1⅛ cup) double cream**

**280ml (½ pint or 1⅛ cup) full fat milk**

**1 vanilla pod**

**2 nettle teabags; remove tea from the bags**

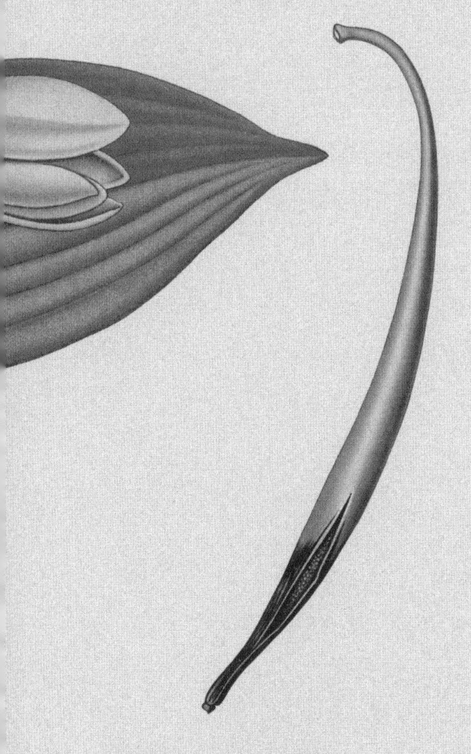

***VANILLA PLANIFOLIA*, VANILLA**

Vanilla is the fruit of an orchid native to Central America and was hard to cultivate in other countries without its specialized pollinator the *Melipona* bee, until people learned to pollinate it by hand.

1. Add the sugar to the egg yolks and whisk until pale and fluffy. Add the cornflour and whisk in well. Set aside for later.
2. Put the cream and milk into a saucepan. Cut the vanilla pod down lengthways and scrape out the seeds with a knife adding them to the cream and milk mixture.
3. Heat the cream and milk mixture until just below boiling, then slowly pour onto the egg and sugar mixture whisking as you pour.
4. After everything has been combined, sieve the mixture into a clean saucepan to remove the vanilla seeds. Add the nettle tea, then on a very low heat, continuously stir the mixture with a wooden spoon until it has thickened slightly. The mixture is ready when you can draw a clear line through it using the back of a spoon. This process will take about 10 minutes.
5. Empty the mixture into a large, shallow freezer-proof container and allow to cool overnight in the fridge.
6. Place in the freezer until it starts to harden. Remove and whisk vigorously with a fork to disperse the ice crystals and keep it smooth. Repeat three times and then leave in the freezer until firm.
7. Alternatively, transfer the mixture into an ice-cream maker and follow the manufacturer's instructions.

# Apple and Nettle Jelly

*For a unique and exciting flavour, pair this delicious sweet, cloudy apple and nettle jelly with a tangy stilton and crunchy oatcakes.*

**MAKES 3 SMALL JARS**

**Approx. 1 kilo (2lb 3oz) of Bramley or other cooking apples**

**560ml (1 pint or 2¼ cups) of nettle tea, made with 2 nettle teabags**

**500g (1lb 2oz or 1¼ cups) granulated sugar**

**2–3 strips of lemon rind**

**Large bunch of fresh nettle tips or young leaves tied together**

**25g (1oz) dried nettles (in a muslin bag)**

**Jelly bag, muslin bag, sterilized pots with lids and waxed jam paper**

1. Wash the apples and cut into rough pieces.
2. Put into a large saucepan and cover with cold nettle tea. Simmer until the apples are soft.
3. Leave to cool. Transfer the contents of the saucepan into a jelly bag and leave to drip into a bowl overnight.
4. Add the sugar to the extracted juice and heat gradually until the sugar is dissolved (approximately 500g of juice to 500g of sugar according to taste).
5. Add the lemon rind, fresh and dried nettles and bring to the boil.
6. Test for setting by removing a small amount to see if it sets on a plate.
7. When ready, remove the lemon rind, nettles and muslin bag. Pour the liquid into sterilized pots, cover with waxed jam paper and leave to cool and set. Seal with a lid when completely cold.

***MALUS DOMESTICA*, HAUTE BONTE**

Apples were once thought to have originated in Britain, but they really came from Central Asia along with many other fruits and nuts.

# Nettle Beer

*Best served ice cold, this pleasant-tasting botanic beer has a lovely spiced kick.*

MAKES 8 PINTS

**900g (2lb) nettle tips or young leaves**

**4.5 litres (1 gallon) water**

**220g (8oz or 1 cup) sugar, brown or demerara sugar work best**

**75g (3oz) ground ginger**

**75g (3oz) fresh yeast**

**1 small piece toast**

**Sealable bottles**

1. In a very large saucepan boil the nettle tops in the water for 30 minutes.
2. Strain the nettles and set aside, retaining the nettle water. Add the sugar to the nettle water and stir to dissolve, and then add the ginger.
3. Pour the nettle water into a large sterile container.
4. Spread the yeast onto the toast and float on the surface of the nettle water. Cover and leave for about 3 days at room temperature. Do not allow the temperature to fluctuate too much as this will ruin the fermentation process.
5. Strain again and divide into screw top beer bottles or sealable wine bottles. The beer can be drunk after about 2 days.

***ZINGIBER OFFICINALE*, GINGER**

Underground stems of ginger allow the plant to spread widely in its native habitat of tropical Asia. A new ginger plant will grow from a tiny piece of stem.

# Grandma's Nettle Wine

*A fine, light, fresh and zingy white wine, with zesty undertones.*

**MAKES 4 TO 5 BOTTLES**

**9 litres (16 pints or 32 cups) water**

**3 carrier bags of nettle tips or young leaves**

**3 unpeeled lemons, thinly sliced**

**1 ginger root, grated**

**2.7kg (6lb or 12 cups) sugar**

**7g (¼oz) packet of yeast**

**1 slice stale toast**

**Air-lock fermentation jar, siphon, bottles with corks**

1. In a large saucepan, cover the nettles with 2 litres (4 pints) of water and bring to the boil.
2. Stir in the lemon and ginger and reduce the heat to a simmer. Leave for 1 hour.
3. Put the sugar in a wine-making vat and strain the cooked warm nettle liquid onto the sugar. Stir until dissolved.
4. Pour in the remaining water and stir. Cover with a cloth and allow to cool.
5. When cool, sprinkle the yeast onto the slice of stale toast and float on the liquid. Re-cover and leave to stand in a warm room for 5 days.
6. Once rested, pour the liquid into a fermentation jar with an air-lock lid and allow fermentation to take place until bubbling ceases. Siphon into sterilized bottles and cork.

***URTICA DIOICA*, COMMON NETTLE**

Nettle stems are used to produce a fibre that is used to make clothing – uniforms during the First World War in Germany were made of nettle fibres because cotton was in short supply.

# Nettle Cordial

*Wonderfully refreshing and sweet, makes an ideal springtime drink.*

MAKES 1 STANDARD BOTTLE

**1kg (2lb 4oz or 4½ cups) granulated sugar**

**40g (1½oz) citric acid**

**500ml (just under 1 pint or 2 cups) boiling water**

**110g (4oz) young blackcurrant leaves**

**110g (4oz) nettle tips or young leaves**

**1 Campden tablet**

1. Place the sugar, citric acid and boiling water into a large saucepan, stir and heat to 60°C (140°F).
2. Add the blackcurrant and nettle leaves and remove immediately from heat. Allow to cool.
3. Cover and leave for a week, stirring daily.
4. Strain and bottle, adding one Campden tablet to the bottle. Alternatively, keep in the fridge and use within one month using one part cordial to ten parts water.

***RIBES NIGRUM*, BLACKCURRANT**

Blackcurrants have high concentrations of anthocyanins. These give the fruit its deep purple colour and are powerful antioxidants considered to have health-giving properties.

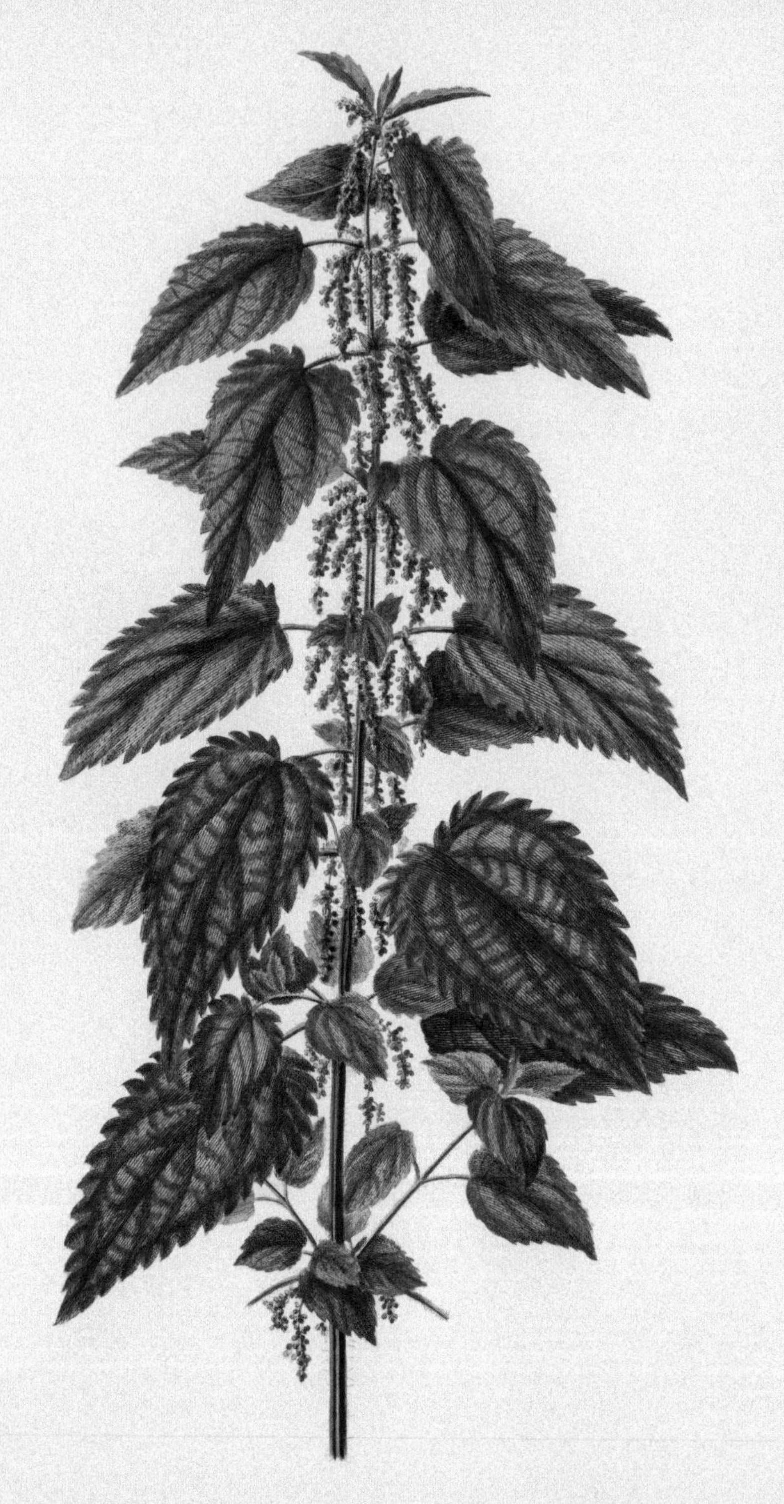

# Apple and Nettle Smoothie

*Creamy and sweet – here is an unexpectedly delicious way to get nettle goodness into your daily diet.*

**MAKES 2 SERVINGS**

**50g (2oz or ⅓ cup) nettle tips or young leaves, blanched (p.7)**

**1 apple, peeled and cored**

**280ml (½ pint or 1⅛ cup) natural yogurt**

**280ml (½ pint or 1⅛ cup) diluted nettle juice or apple juice**

**6 ice cubes**

1. Blend the ingredients at high-speed in a blender until smooth.
2. You can add more juice to make a thinner drink or more yoghurt for a thicker texture.

***URTICA DIOICA*, COMMON NETTLE**

The caterpillars of several species of butterfly, such as the peacock and the small tortoise shell, only eat nettle leaves, despite their sting.

# Nettle, Apple and Grape Smoothie

*With a refreshingly light flavour, this smoothie will keep you satisfied and cool on a hot day.*

**MAKES 2 SERVINGS**

**200g (7oz) seedless grapes**

**50g (2oz) nettle tips or young leaves, blanched (p.7)**

**1 apple, peeled and cored**

**280ml (½ pint or 1⅛ cup) apple juice**

**6 ice cubes**

1 To make this smoothie, simply blend all the ingredients in a blender until smooth.

2 Add more ice if needed.

***VITIS VINIFERA*, BLACK HAMBURG**

Grapes were first domesticated in the Mediterranean region from wild plants whose fruits were probably eaten by birds and mammals. They were spread all over Europe by the Romans who took them to the far-flung corners of their Empire.

# Simple Pizza Dough Mix

*An easy dough for beautifully crispy pizzas.*

MAKES 3–4 THIN PIZZA BASES

**300g (10oz or 1¼ cups) strong white bread flour**

**1 tsp salt**

**200ml (¼ pint or ¾ cup) lukewarm water**

**1 tsp golden caster sugar**

**1 tsp dried yeast**

**1 tbsp olive oil**

1. Sieve the flour and salt into a large bowl, and then make a well.
2. Put the lukewarm water, sugar, yeast, and olive oil into a jug and leave for 3 minutes to activate yeast.
3. Pour the liquid into the flour well and mix slowly with your fingers or a wooden spoon.
4. When the dough has all come together, tip it out onto a floured board and knead for 5 minutes until it is soft and springy.
5. Roll the dough out to your desired thickness or thinness. Note, when cooking, the dough will double in thickness.

# Index

Page numbers in *italic* refer to illustration captions.

# Acknowledgements

With their kind permission, the recipes in this book have been inspired by original recipes from the copyright owners as listed. All additional recipes are the author's own.

**PP.14–15 CREAM OF NETTLE SOUP**
**PP.70–71 GRANDMA'S NETTLE WINE**
*Vitality Magazine*, www.vitalitymagazine.com

**PP.16–17 ASPARAGUS AND NETTLE SOUP**
**PP.38–39 NETTLE PASTA**
Saffron Restaurant, www.saffronrestauranttruro.co.uk

**PP.20–21 POTATO AND NETTLE SOUP**
*Little Red Gooseberries – Organic Recipes from Penrhos*, Daphne Lambert, Orion Books, 2001

**PP.26–27 NETTLE HAGGIS**
**PP.68–69 NETTLE BEER**
www.selfsufficientish.com/main/

**PP.32–33 NETTLE KAIL**
*Scottish Regional Recipes*, Catherine Brown, Penguin Books, 1983

**PP.34–35 NETTLE FRITTATA**
*Chez Panisse Cafe Cookbook*, Alice Waters, William Morrow Cookbooks, 2004

**PP.36–37 NETTLE MASH WITH ROAST BROCCOLI AND SESAME SEEDS**
**PP.40–41 NETTLE RAVIOLI**
Daphne Lambert, www.greencuisinetrust.org

**PP.46–47 SAUSAGE AND NETTLE CALZONE**
Terese Allen, http://www.organicvalley.coop/

**PP.50–51 STINGING NETTLE PESTO**
www.gourmetsleuth.com

**PP.58–59 GRANNY BELLS SCONES**
www.grannybells.com

**PP.72–73 NETTLE CORDIAL**
www.thorncroftdrinks.co.uk

Every effort has been made to contact and accurately credit all copyright holders. If we have been unsuccessful, we apologize and welcome corrections for future reprints.

Please note, all website addresses are subject to change.